ELIJAH FED BY RAVENS

ELIJAH FED BY RAVENS

_____

Kristina Erny

ISBN 979-8-9879514-5-3

Cover art by Kristina Erny
Cover and Interior design by Sarah Christolini
Author photo by Katie Eckhardt, used with permission.

Excerpt from "Mass for the Day of St. Thomas Didymus" from SELECTED POEMS OF DENISE LEVERTOV, copyright © 1982 by Denise Levertov. Reprinted by permission of New Directions Publishing Corp.

"Aubade" from A GARDEN IN KENTUCKY, copyright © 1995 by Jane Gentry. Reprinted by permission of LSU Press.

Library of Congress Cataloging-in-Publication Data
Name: Erny, Kristina, author.
Title: Elijah fed by ravens / Kristina Erny.
Description: Scottsdale, AZ: Solum Literary Press, 2023.
Identifiers: LCCN 2023946947
ISBN: 979-8-9879514-5-3 (print)
ISBN: 979-8-9879514-6-0 (ePub)
Subjects: BISAC: POETRY / General / Subjects & Themes - Inspirational and Religious / American - General
LC record available at https://lccn.loc.gov/2023946947

Solum Literary Press
2055 E Hampton Ave, 235
Mesa, AZ 85204
(480) 371-9053

for B, E, M, & Ph

*I believe and
interrupt my belief with
doubt. I doubt and
interrupt my doubt with belief. Be,
belovèd, threatened world.*

— Denise Levertov, "Mass for the Day of St. Thomas Didymus"

At daybreak a crow's hard cry
breaks apart the darkness,
which disappears black
feather by black feather.

— Jane Gentry, "Aubade," A Garden in Kentucky

Now Elijah the Tishbite, from Tishbe in Gilead, said to Ahab, "As the Lord, the God of Israel, lives, whom I serve, there will be neither dew nor rain in the next few years except at my word." Then the word of the Lord came to Elijah: "Leave here, turn eastward and hide in the Kerith Ravine, east of the Jordan. You will drink from the brook, and I have directed the ravens to supply you with food there."

So he did what the Lord had told him. He went to the Kerith Ravine, east of the Jordan, and stayed there. The ravens brought him bread and meat in the morning and bread and meat in the evening, and he drank from the brook.

1 Kings 17: 1-5

Contents

Notes

Many poems in this book take inspiration, borrow images, and steal plot points from the stories of Elijah in 1 Kings 17, 18, 19 and 2 Kings 2. 1 and 2 Kings were most likely written down by a man named Jeremiah who also wrote a book named after himself, as well as one appropriately named Lamentations. A reader may enjoy looking at the original text alongside these poems, but that is not necessary to understand the poems' meaning. There are also poems in this book which reference the birth of Christ, which appears in several different versions in the books of Matthew, Mark, Luke, and John. The translation of the Holy Bible that I consulted and spent time with was Today's New International Version which includes the chapter heading "Elijah Fed by Ravens," which I also have stolen, and am noting here.

"In the Days Before" is indebted to Amelia Martens, *The Spoons in the Grass are There to Dig a Moat.*

"The Way to Horeb" is for Edie Moon; "Beloved" is for Youngen Lee; "Mite" is for Moses Eugene & Ephraim Wallace, "SHUTTLE" is for Phyllina Sal; "On the Eve of our Fourteenth Wedding Anniversary" and "On the Eve of our Sixteenth Wedding Anniversary" are for Benjamin.

"Manda" is an ekphrastic poem in response to Brian Paumier's "Act of Faith" an artwork I saw displayed at 21c Hotel in Lexington, Kentucky, July 2021

"Elijah Fed by Ravens," "The Widow," "The Widow at Zarephath," "Obadiah Speaks to Elijah," "Horeb, Mountain of the Lord," "To Heaven in a Whirlwind," "Anticipation," and "Agnus Dei" are all acrostic poems. "We Came Running," "The Way to Horeb," and "Beloved" are sonnets. "In the Beginning" is a contrapuntal and "Cause" is an abecedarian.

Some of the poems in this book are resurrections of other poems. This form involves using the original poem as a sort of word bank, playing at a whole word anagram. In a true resurrection, all words from the original poem must be used and none can be repeated if they were not repeated in the original poem. They are reassembled into something new. A new body. A reassemblage is a resurrection. See language make a poem into a body, see that poem breathe, live, then die as the page turns. Now see the body revived into a new way of thinking, remade to live again, reanimated, but not the same. A resurrection. Just as Elijah raised the widow's son back from the dead. Just as Elijah himself was brought back from the coffin he had built for himself under the broom tree. Just as Elijah's ghost stood with Jesus in the garden. The form reaches out toward the content.

The following poems are resurrections of other poems in this collection:

"The Ravens" is a resurrection of "Hear Me," "Elijah and the Widow" is a resurrection of "The Widow," "Obadiah and Elijah" is a resurrection of "Obadiah Speaks to Elijah," "The Lord" is a resurrection of "Horeb, Mountain of the Lord," "Teach Us" is a resurrection of "What the Trees Teach Us," and "praxis, too" is a resurrection of Wendy Xu's "praxis."

Acknowledgements and Gratitude

I am thankful for the following literary magazines and anthologies which gave these poems a home.

"A Sign" appeared in Episcopal Charities' Lenten Reader, Year C, Spring 2022.

"Cause," "praxis, too," and "In the Days Before" appeared in *TRANSOM*, Issue 15, Fall 2022.

"Elijah and the Widow" and "Hear Me" (as "Elijah Fed by Ravens") appeared as earlier versions in *Blackbird*, Fall 2019, Vol. 18, No. 2.

"Elijah on Mt. Carmel" was a finalist for *Ruminate's* Broadside Poetry Prize, 2020.

"Elijah on Mt. Carmel" appeared in *Episcopal Charities' Lenten Reader, Year B*, Spring 2021.

"Elijah Fed by Ravens" and "The Way to Horeb" appeared in *Yemassee*, Issue 25.1, Spring 2018.

"Gloria" appeared as "Resurrection" in the CIVA show and publication, *Again & Again*, paired with Keith Barker's photograph "Stone of Help."

"Good Friday" (as "Bad Friday") appeared in *Rattle*, Summer 2022.

"Mary Ruefle Told Me" appeared in *Kansas City Voices*, Spring 2022.

"Nobody's Mother" appeared in *Rabbit Catastrophe*, Fall 2019.

"O God," "Cast," and "On the Eve of Our Fourteenth Wedding Anniversary" appeared in *Many Nice Donkeys*, Issue 2.

"Obadiah Speaks to Elijah" and "Elijah & Obadiah" appeared in *Episcopal Charities' Lenten Reader, Year A*, Spring 2020.

"On to Horeb" appeared in *Free State Review*, Summer 2019.

"SHUTTLE" is forthcoming in Tupelo Press's *The Last Milkweed* Anthology.

"The Lord Appears to _____" is introduction poem to the CIVA show and publication, *Again & Again*, paired with Leticia Huckaby's artwork, *Ask, Seek, Knock*.

"What the Trees Teach Us" and "Horeb, Mountain of the Lord" appeared in *Solum Journal* Winter 2022.

"Witness" appeared in the *Sonora Review*, April 2021.

I'm so thankful for very smart, generous, and beautiful people who spoke life into this book and helped to shape these poems:

Thank you to Sublimity City poets Kristi Maxwell, Jessica Farquhar, John James, V. Joshua Adams, Ann DeVilbiss, Danielle Smalley, Kristen Miller, Emma Aprile, and Ken Walker. Thank you to Lexington poets Carrie Green and Jeremy Paden. Thank you to Shanghai poets Andres Sanabria, Ben Beach, Jacob Luo, and Sam King. Thank you to David Arnold. Thank you to Joy Priest, Dorianne Laux, Tarfia Faizullah, Ada Limón, Ilya Kaminsky, and Ross Gay. Thank you to the poets and writers in my cohort at The University of Arizona MFA and for the teachings of Barbara Cully, Alison Hawthorne Deming, Marcia Hurlow, Jane Miller, Edie Moon, Steve Orlen, and Richard Siken. Thank you to my colleagues in the English department at Asbury University. Thank you to Susanna Childress. Thank you to Tupelo Press for selecting me as a participant for 30/30 in 2016 during which the first poems were written. Thank you to the good people at Solum Literary Press for giving these poems a home.

Thank you to my sisterwife Katie Eckhardt, first, best reader. Thank you to a sisterhood which has loved, fed, and sustained me: Katelyn, Cami, Sarah, Kristi, Emily, Kim, Lanie, Kristen, Youngen, Corrie, Christie, Carol, Jamie, Lisa, Alisa, Anna Lee, Katie.

Thank you to my aunties Edie Moon and Jennie Purvis, poets themselves, who showed me a way into poetry.

Thank you to my Oma and Papa, who took our family on a journey both physical and spiritual from which we have never turned back. Thank you to my ancestors Wallace and Betty Rehner, and Les and Pat Ike, whose dedication and love shaped those who shaped me. To the Raders, the Rehners, the Moons, the Purvises, the Ikes, the Ernys, my family, thank you.

Thank you to my in-laws, Paul and Jenny Erny, Christie and Nick Felker, Amber and Milton Garcia, and my nephews and nieces, who love me and have always let me be me.

Thank you to my mom and dad, Helen and JP Rader, who are my biggest cheerleaders. To Paul and Hannah Rader and to Brittney and Jesse Fields, and their sweet boys, who have loved me and put up with me from the beginning. *Saranghae.* Stink thanks you.

To my students strewn all around the world, and for sacred spaces we made together in Whiteland, Tucson, Daejeon, Indianapolis, Seoul, Wilmore, and now Shanghai. I love you. These poems were written alongside you. It is the making that makes us. Thank you.

To Ephraim, Moses, and Phyllina, these poems have grown alongside you and whether you like it or not, you are in every one. Thank you for loving me and making me who I am. You are the best books of poetry. I love you one thousand million loves.

To Benjamin, best of lovers, best of men. Blessings, blessings, a thousand blessings. I love you. Amen.

Thank you, God, great Mystery, for love, for poems, and for being okay with our questions.

ELIJAH FED BY RAVENS

On the Eve of our Fourteenth Wedding Anniversary

Wind, again, outside. We aren't supposed to write
       of the weather, or the moon, wry blue ash tips,
       once-loved sky. But what else is so new
it deserves a second glance? I peeled

       curtains back like a bandaid and saw no one.
Heard once that a tornado sounds like a train.
Our daughter grinds her teeth. Rain, rain,
       our toe-up yard sogged to shambles. Every hour

another flicker of bad news. We hiss
       it's sad, real sad. So you chew
       up our house and spit it out
as a chrysalis. When you exhale

       that's when we'll hatch. Rebirth's a bitch.
What a callous story: transcontinental move,
low-paying job, opportunity's snapped branch, regret.
       The solution slaps like a wet dress.

I can only see as far as the yard, its honeysuckled edge.
       Are you even listening? Have a heart. It's not even spring yet,
       and I'm sneezing, water dripping from both my eyes.
I swear I heard a dog bark somewhere outside.

What the Trees Teach Us

In the middle and all through,
the trees. Old whirring things.

And in the in-between between
their leaves, time, pinched up.

What falls is not forgotten,
only traded for another sun.

Who else spoke the language
of death from life first?

And did anyone see the green thread
trail into the dirt,

then trellis up
as morning glory?

Elijah Fed by Ravens

i.
Even the whisper
leaves the black feathers
inchoate. Rustled
jump-leap gathering
another stick, a
hope caught there under

first scuffle. Feathered
eyes feather-sore; the
days waiting, days gone.

Before the raven comes:
yawn and brook the tiniest

relève of pebble. Cave.
Anger sifts, shifts, no
vapor of it left.

Elijah opens
nocturne of hunger, a
secondary mouth.

ii.
black feather, black mouth
black teeth, black shine

open black, black cave
ripples in black brook

black water, black thoughts
black sunshine

back burns black to the rock
black underside of leaves

black feather, black feathers
black flight, black shine of feathers

in morning light
black grit of black nails

scrape of black rocks
the black of black moss

the future is figment
so eat up given bread

lift up another head
what is sustenance

passed from black beaks
black bread feeds

a black fire in our belly
backed by a black and holy God

In the Days Before

In the days before the actual end there were many smaller heartbreaks. Moths ceased their incessant tapping against screen doors. Cows shivered and dropped to their knees. Milk was poured casually down the drain.

At the edge of the field, a gyre of common starlings, kudzu like a plastic bag over the forest's face.

Once there was a tree so stalwart and wide a family of five circled round and the children slapped its trunk with joy. Under the pavement, there was a field ripe with wildflowers, in the field, foxes, instead of vinyl siding.

A person used to be able to split through the husk and know there would be seeds.

Kyrie

Overhead the cloud
      split like a melon.

O banged up Light, O color
      leeched from *please*,
      have mercy.

Please help us be
      perfected, see this body
      winnowed down to wafer.
      How our tongues reach out.

Understand that we live somewhere between hide
      and seek. Wonder
      if our crow will
      ever come.

Will we witness it once?
      Or will that be enough?

I'll take
      what I can get.

In the Beginning

it began in   disappointment,
a loose grip, hands   perpetual,
shaking, eyes   unfocused, a blur &
sun-spots at the   center. its black
tint, the core, if   you can call it that.

Elijah's vision of old   black feathers, vision of
dark nest a   denouement, a

merciful conclusion, release
thirsty for re-   lease. more mercy
burned black feathers   to start a fire

black smoke from the   black fire. it proves
provision isn't all   tasty, but also

        I can call it

        good

Hear Me

Listen, you caught the raven's
beak, couldn't stand the wait.

You took the meat before
you were ready. Brook dried,

and the dried-up brook had rocks,
a bottom unfit for baking bread.

The story comes later. You couldn't wait
and meat was there. But

you still didn't believe,
you saw the sun-through-leaves,

the air was dry, and a sun
shone. You cannot be happy.

You ask yourself why
at least once a day.

At least you are outside, at least
you have someone who rubs oil

on your neck. The brook
is a word saying *go, go, you can't stay*

here. Listen, you catch the raven
by the stem and force him

to tell you the truth;
his laugh sounds like dried leaves

or what we call *the fall*, packed
under piles, the names of trees still

escape you. It's okay, you can call
yourself ungrateful as you swallow

down the bread, the meat, before
you get up, before you can leave.

Cause

If not atom, then air-conditioning,
if not baby scream, then boo-boos, dead bees,
if not sun-screened coral, then incubator, cheatgrass, curdled milk,
if not clogged ducts, then a dementor, or dog poop,
if not E. coli, then Easter baskets, or eczema, or empire,
if not friends, then their frenzy,
if not gringos, then growth hormones,
if not hair with rat's nests, then horses beaten dead,
if not imposters, the internet, sharp incisors,
if not jackals, then jokesters,
if not kudzu, then lack of kindness,
if not personal limit, then destruction of liminal space,
if not meatloaf, then broken mitosis,
if not niceness, then a child's nautical death, thin and never-ending
        cord of bubbles, rising up,
if not organ failure, then oregano, origami, false optimism,
        pustule, permissiveness,
loss of quilt patterns, too many quaaludes,
if not reality tv, then risk assessment,
if not starling, then single-syllable response,
if not burnt toast, then endless talking,
if not umbrella, then umbilical cord,
if not varicose, then only one version of events,
if not waste, then our want,
if not xenophobes, then extravagant spending,
if not yesterday, or the lack of the color yellow,
if not zealots, then what made us all zeroes?

Gloria

Lord of empty bowl and thrift store spoon,
of soil, of paint-flecked arms.
Lord of the mossed live oak, of blank paper, of lobe.

You are gingko leaf, its yellow tone,
an egg feather-stuck, a room. The lingering scent
of myrrh, of aloe, folded strips of linen,
cast light across the sandy floor of a tomb.

You live deep in ginger's bite, snow's precision,
the seed the wildflower's thrown.

You are the Lord of all expectant breath:
height, cloud, vapor, mist.

You are the Lord of what's been bitten down,
what's dormant, the remaindered, the paused.

Molecule's God, salamander's God, ragweed's
God, Lord of stones.
Lord of green-bellied toad's
burble and spit.

Of broad-winged hawks,
of weather and wings, of wood mites' burrows,
of whistles, of small things.

We balk, Lord, at how you nestle deep: our bulb, our bee,
juice, the Spirit of pear, the shadow of the dimple,
what's under every ripple of the creek.

Lord of the hitch, the lob, the blink, the kiss, the shake.
Lord who rose, who wakes;

who lets us sleep, who satiates.

In our palms, cerebrum, nostrils, wrists,
your Spirit lives. What we miss,
forgive. In our liminal lives,
share with us your margins today.

The Ravens
a resurrection of "Hear Me"

Yourself swallow, leave, escape.
You call, you can pack piles, meat,

sounds, under trees. Fall, you
ungrateful, forced truth-teller.

Listen, Elijah, go oil your neck,
the brook is dried. Wait for a happy

word. You stay here, stem. At least it's day
outside, at least you're happy. Laugh,

you cannot be a sun. You can dry up
for baking. You had rocks, you took meat,

you were ready in the beak of the brook.
Listened, caught. You stand; you wait.

The Widow
1 Kings 17:7-24

Even ravens need crusts, something.
Left behind, everyone left.
It begs the question—
jar bottom,
a flag of surrender?
Hostile, hand-held, the haze.

Always the tone;
never the ringing.
Drives her

to the pot where the flour is
hoped for, hidden— & then, his face in the doorway— *have,*
eat— Yes, we are eaten— still a future, grim. O,

won't you come in.
I would have baked the cake &
died. Instead, she performs, participates in
onerous miracle, & tomorrow
wakes up, blinking, hoary film under her nails.

Ravens

crow old
crow stole
crow saw
dough stowed

told man
sold man bold ask woman
lack woman   cracked
knack of men

plan can stand
tend towards
win
            wend
mend
            we
friend

neat
            meat

beastgreet

heat   so weak

meek must seek
must teach

trust
            us

deep
    stuck

your
muck

Elijah and the Widow
a resurrection of "The Widow"

Left ravens, crust of something.

> Begs to eat, begs question.
> (Hostile)

Baked & tomorrow— *Wake up! You died!*

Won't she surrender the jar bottom. *Where's the flour hid?*

> Participate in a hoary hope, Everyone.

Then,

his face the tone
> always ringing—

Driven to doorway,
> to pot,
> to a future grim.

O, I would have a miracle
> onerous, always eaten blinking.

> Perform her need, her held hand's a future.

> Instead,
> > where the flour is.

Credo
1 Kings 19

The drum major's impulse
      is to hit, run. While reading these stories, his hand
becomes my hand, some rapt pendulum, a held out
      metronome. We are connected,

me and Elijah, brethren. The tattoo
      of religion's drums. The moment
I move a muscle, some imperceptible string
      has a hold of my ankle, my neck.

We organize, by beating, a faith
      that's rhythmic. Human feet are the strongest
measurement. In these stories, he serves
      as our conductor. We hear the music

and beg to be led out of our endless desert,
      (while afraid, while trembling),
while our bags, bags, bags, balance on our heads.
      Because others beat us there. They have already

taken themselves to the camp's edge of what's human, possible.
      (see: scapegoat) (read: origin sin)
My whole life I've listened to that age-old call and response.
      We are waiting for answers. I think

we are meant to hold up our hands empty,
      believe that what we need will come down.

The Widow at Zarephath
1 Kings 17:17-24

Then he asked so I gave.
He said we would be blessed because his words were
earning the Lord's keep. Outside, a

wasted land, baked
idiomatic as a sunset. Slowly
drying up, my boy. I want a boy
ornery and restless as a snake. Elijah, the prophet, full, fed, but even
        after his blessing, my boy's
windows shut hard with a stone. I begged, so for us he made Death
        this time

an alibi, a wafer taken back from the mouth, palmed halfway into
tasteless mush. This house would have been over,

zeroed. I hungered for a return. Elijah is a man and thus
allowed to wander, arrive in the nick of time.
Red, what comes after that nick.
Emancipated now, my boy's flesh is pinked up like a Bikfaya
peach. A mother's relief. Now I am left to
hazard his inevitable second death,
adventure with survivor's guilt. I stir it into the starter, sugar into
        yeasty foam.
Tinker with how it flavors what we'll be tasting. We're alive.
Hallelujah clings bitter to the teeth, tinged with all that stays dead.
        People are profitless margins,
        read into the blanks between the lines.

What I hear is

*you've wasted
your days.*

I refuse that sentence,
each impartial letter.

What's the part
parallel
to
perfection,   only,
            only, only the
            one,

            this one here...

You know,

*I draw my own
circles around trees.*

*I can dream in two
colors.*

I said, *I want to know.*

I said,
        feed me.

I said, *this isn't good enough*

It's simple.

So often we just fail to dig;

Hope's a shovel made for this.
       it sings:

I still got my hands;
I still got my neck.

Obadiah Speaks to Elijah
1 Kings 18:1-15

O yes, blame me. You've
been in hiding so long you've forgotten what you look like. You're
a man who emerges while I stoop into every
driveway scanning tufts, less grass.
Isn't that great! Here you
are! A self-made hero masked in
hysteria. Where were you when we needed

a man who could speak? A man who inches
      into the right time, right place.
          No, I'm thrilled,
          Elijah.
No need for backchecks, but can I keep an I.D.? Your beard's
      got black feathers.
      Proof enough. See
dust fill our bowls.

Even our children know how to make
little mud cakes. They try to smile while chewing.
I was called. I stayed. I fell on my face for you,
justified. I thought I was saved. You're the prophet, can't you see
after we end in surrender,
how easy it could be to run again?

22

Witness

Stand right there. I'm tired of bad poems about
nature. I'm over motherhood and cook

tops and sweeping up again and again.
I want to walk outside under the beamed

overpass without thinking about all
the ways it could fall on my head.

I want kids who listen dammit. I've tried
grappling with issues that are much too

complicated for me to understand.
Yesterday, I got over it, and yet

today, it's the same. For example, it would be
nice to sip tea and not burn my lip, take

a warm bath, rose Epsom salts, a sheet mask.
Some believe today will be better than

yesterday, better than the day before
but mostly we are nostalgic for

some dim but tender circle of light.
I am witness to my own life. So what.

I eat memory post-dinner like a mint.
And sometimes I hum, am human.

Obadiah & Elijah
a resurrection of "Obadiah Speaks to Elijah"

Blame you've been hiding.
                                        Run, man, I thought.
A forgotten man, after scanning self as hero,
came to where you were, again.

Black beard,
little bowl, our dust
called "prophet" now.

                                        Yes, children too make cakes.
Check your id, the ego,

                                        we smile
                how to be?

                                        Our fall while justified.

You'll merge *here* into time,
...place...you'll see.

Thrill was Elijah, who is grass?

You know right, *right*?
                                        O, it was for me.

No, you're a   *can't,*   *no.*

                                        I stoop tufted, got feathers easy,
inches needed even now.

I could speak:

every man I know could

and

How could I keep proof
      less me,

while the long way
drives my greatness.

And made into who?
I,   *you,*   *they*
(all in on it)

You look like a *you* in hiding,
back for enough?

What are we?

I'm chewing upon need.

Stayed surrender isn't that.

When filled,
I end in mud.

Can the face you see save?

Sanctus

Holy, Holy, Holy Lord
Shod in Earth's delight
Sole he, Sole she, Sole we, Lord
Clod of Testament's right

Leaven birth times, birth fall of a story
Hosanna in the highest, manna when its driest
Blessed are We who drum in the shade of the storm
Hosanna, manna's riot.

Images lag, millennia
                    between
                        messages
shot from immortal
brain

Power small and snuck in,
        a splinter

Name of
        the Other

whisper of

        what is constantly
given

sometimes taken

        (so they say)

Elijah on Mt. Carmel
1 Kings 18:16-39

It is another morning where
we are zipped up heavy.

The dross of nightfall
& yellow-dust coats our lungs.

So, too, we all awakened:
is this enough? Suppose

the trench is dug. We few
remain, & we stand as

sentries to *I forget what,*
but we are here. Press

play on today's prayer for
fire. That meat you

halved, quartered, waits
for its roasting, its

chance to burn. I woke
and came to see. I woke

and am standing near.

Ravens, Mt. Carmel

crow meet   meat

heat
      wait   hate bait

      baal   late
stale mates

stand
         hands

kneel wheel pile   rocks

talk
talk
        while
            miles
higher
spill
    cut
        the guts
a slogan open

wait   wait
    wait   wait

make
pyre
    pale,   dire

cut   wire
trust   us

        black thought
                        laugh's
                trough
crackle
tough
blood's   enough

pray
        slay say

stake
take
        bowed

        see
                cloud
where is
God

God

nods

The Way to Horeb
1 Kings 19:1-9

Arise, arise, the journey is too great

for you alone to master. Muster bread

from the bloody beaks of angels, & eat

standing or with your head on a rock. Say

nothing, just go & keep on going till you are

spent & burned up, crispy as meat, as leaf.

This is a life well meant, traveling far

& wide, investing near. No one can grieve

you this· *you were awake.* Your mouth drank

what the brook would give when it would give it.

Black feathers stuff your pillows; your teeth sink

right down to the bone. You cannot sit

still even for a minute. This is gift,

whip. You say holy, and you mean it.

Ravens

      crows know
            bereft

what's
    left

man
      slept

      cleft rot

      fought   rock

men

stalk
slake

        sing the wake

cling & bring

        swoop

        in loops

whine
        shhhh

    win

glisten
     when
listen

the brook   had hooks   we

     looked

you

begin

     man
         again

     stuffed

     ears

leer

fear blink   what they miss

heaven's kiss

       all alone

atone

one   little palmed
stone

       lamb
come

empty
space

       room

womb

thin win

we
     din

       savor   men

Confession

we open our hands to see blood on them
shrug first one shoulder then the next

and half a blame flames imperceptible

then

we swallow neatly
our nightly whiskey

our eyes roam to all the flickering lights
    (the sky's red above the city)

and belatedly we think something might be
burning

how can we live with ourselves
when everything has so many consequences

in our hand is a glass that's half empty

    on the news the glass was blown to pieces

    and
    thus
    empty

ruined by someone else   someone we probably know

On to Horeb

1 Kings 19:3-9

Lo, the trees within the trees are moaning.
The rocks within the rocks have fouled. Broom tree
umbrellas above you, human. Tones of
desert, gloaming life. Do you think this frees
you? ...relinquishing, after you've waited?
After all you've seen? You ran, who always
run. Had sustenance anyone would crave.
You forget you looked seven times sideways
through your knees. You saw the cloud as a man's
hand rising from the sea. Remember? You
saw the sky blacken, and its drench. The land's wan
sinews. *I've had enough,* poor body pooled
in shade. I'm tired, too. I am here to tell you,
get up. Eat this bread, push through.

Good Friday

I put on my good
lipstick in preparation
to mourn,

and outside
three redbuds pink out
like Magdalenes
holding cherry margaritas,
each cup full
of blossom rimmed
with salt sun.

The Kid Bible
doesn't show
any blood.

And when my daughter
asks about the crown
of thorns, I tell her
the truth,
complete
with whips, nails,
long drips of bright
blood.

I make her cry, thinking
about Baby Jesus
nailed at right angles,
pierced in the side,
the shape his baby
body made, dangling
there.

No, I say, *he wasn't a baby.*
He'd grown up to do this.

But why'd they have to nail him,
she says, *it would hurt.*

Her eyes grow glossy, her lips fall, pinch.

Because they wanted to kill him like a criminal,
and this is how criminals were killed back then.

But it's not fair,
he didn't do anything wrong,
didn't they know
that he was good?

Her brows push together,
begin clenching
and unclenching their fists.

I know, baby,
that's the point

Feeling good, my head nods,
I'm doing good, she's getting it.

When's Bad Friday, she says.

After a pause,
the tree behind her
shakes, spills its cocktail
across the lawn.

Suddenly, she reaches out
and clasps my cheeks

with both her palms,
kisses me hard
on the mouth.

Then she rubs her index finger
slowly across her bottom lip,
looks down, smiling,

and she shows me,
it's red.

Horeb, Mountain of the Lord
1 Kings 19:9-13

How many times can we pass by?

Open years Elijah, into the day before the crows, your own
red creek bottom—Dry-stone fears that you can't hear us

Elijah, wait with your
back to the hurricane—We are

moved to what burns you

O, get your head out from
under the rock

Note small differences in
temperature, the hair on your arms seismic, standing up
again like it did the last time

Isn't there always a last time?

Note the way the air stills and the ravens
                              become contemplative

What they question
How they know us

Elijah. They have
reached into their tiny minds and have bowed down already,
ever dark, even on this forsaken and holy

transom

Here we are—Why are we still here?

Eat this whisper, a wafer of our kindness

Lean your lobe over and place it
on the ground
                    It is best to
reach back into the vacuum and shut off your own
devices, black them out until you are

melted down, tucked in,
eager, ready to be threaded out,

taken once again into our palms—Who better than

Elijah to be consoled here and now; he runs away and whines,
lists all the ways we've failed him,
inches closer and closer to the edge of the cliff,
just cloak, just feathers, such
a miniscule
human ear

A Sign

Five crows the size of my torso,
feathers like pupils or outer
space, shined over
a styrofoam Cane's chicken container,
balled up paper napkins, trashcans
by the tennis court toppled
in yesterday's wind.

Five crows means one for each
of us. I didn't see them at first
on the hillside, my walk to work.

It was early, a winter morning.
A sky stippled white, not yet fully
light. I had been asking for this.

Some sign, some gust, some guess
at what I should or shouldn't do
with my life—the sudden mess
of black birds.

Of course, I counted the birds.

I tape take-out cookie fortunes
to bulletin boards. I burn
incense, consult the sky,
watch the way the lake
plays its light.

I quiz the ditch for what God
might be saying.

Today,

the honeylocust had already shook
loose almost all of its seeds,
and the sky was mostly
static.

Five crows hopped together
on the grass, then mine took off,
followed by the others, chicken tender
in beak, french-fry in claw,

Ha-ha, ha-ha

I'm listening, I yelled.

The crows, already far out
above the soccer field, disappeared
into anonymous blue,

having already eaten,
having moved
on.

The Lord
a resurrection of "Horeb, Mountain of the Lord"

We question time's hurricane,
our hair threaded to the cliff,
until lobe and transom console closer,
the vacuum whines in eager ground.

We are many, our us, our own mountain.
He's best bowed, tucked into *here*.
Why here? This is *of* us: a last note
melted down, then you're over it, on your own.

Open Elijah year by ear.
List Elijah and kindness.
Eat inches better than Elijah.
Rock Elijah for the last time.

It's just... we are *already* in the human place.
We are already air, what stands up still burning.
They wait to hear, they run to the dry lean,
the miniscule creek, cloak forsaken devices

into failed takeaways. Isn't that the red way now?
Back off. Closer bottomed out, down and such,
just once again. Whose fears armed
like you did? How tiny can be seismic.

Come back, be reached in here again,
contemplative, small even, different.
You can't get your mind out from under
your head. *Lord*. O Horeb,

still moved to pass black whispers, you know
the crow notes, i.e. the holy temperature of ravens.

How we've reached out to wafer time, shut the dark
stone, the day always in a palm's edge, a feather.

On the Eve of our Sixteenth Anniversary

We are frothy with longing like we've always been,
like a bathtub we stepped out of, stepped back in.

Who decides our life? I saw turkey vultures
out our window riding the wind a couple of days

ago, and I was jealous of them. You know how it is:
a season of trees bent over almost in half.

Jessamine's wind lipped our chimney
yet they were so still, hovering, like paintings

of birds. Under them, the field was a countertop,
cows spilled like peppercorns behind paper cutouts

of trees. I breathed in and out
while their slow, controlled orbit looked like,

I could swear under my breath,
joy. Over the wind, I could hear nothing

but the blackness of buzzards scraping
their tender circles against the sky.

Manda

after Brian Paumier, "Act of Faith"

The desert a lonely stretch of pale blue
followed by a yellow slap.

He remembers dying not once, but twice.

A child among the chaparral, the ocean
a plate he loved to balance imagination on.

The rope of a grey mare.
She reared up suddenly,

his grandfather shaved in the shade.

The next time he died it was in Iraq,
his beard dust-riddled and grey.

His stars were merely stickers then,
he saw clearly the glitter red, white, and blue.

Where do the glitter star stickers go
after they've failed as the hero's halo?

A black lamb nuzzled his face, butterflies landed
on his eyes. They say death is a door that locks

on the other side. He knocked and miraculously

she answered. He knocked again and Guadalupe
burst into black birds, and he was quiet, dropped
his hand.

She gave him permission to turn around,
to come back from the other side.

Elegy

we carry each other
there, on wagons
made of scrap, in the backseat
of the van, on couch cushions,
on hammocks, on hospice beds,
under piles of knotted
afghans

we listen close
from the next room,
to lungs breathing
their last,

we text daily, weekly,
hold a hand, squeeze it,

when we press our faces closer
our spirit fogs glass,

when we sing a favorite
hymn before eating
touching at the table
hands not yet gone quiet

like animals, we grasp
loose skin in our teeth
and heave up to release
our beloved from cold snow,

like babies, we nestle
them in the crook
of our arm, we say
        just drink a little, please

take one more bite
we open their lips
with our little spoons,

> *you'll need your strength*

we say, *it's okay,*
> *it's almost time and we*
> *can only go part-way*

> *when you get there*
> *there will be a black door*
> *some say is ringed*
> *with yellow light*

> *you'll need to be brave*
> *to open it but we'll lean*
> *our shoulders in*

> *and place your feet upon them*

Teach Us

a resurrection of "What the Trees Teach Us"

Death traded the pinched middle

What old things in leaves

Life in and through anyone else

From first trail then up

Trees who spoke and did see

Trellis morning, all glory

In the forgotten language, only sun

Time trees up between green whirring

What is not another

Dirt as thread between falls

Benedictus

Blessèd are you who answer the prophet's knock
Blessèd are you as you continue to take stock

Blessèd window, blessed jest,
blessed sunshine, what's second best

Your blessèd fingers licked all the way clean
Blessèd temptation to make the self seen

Blessèd are you who cannot make up your mind
Blessèd those who suck on the rind

Blessèd the ones terrified of death
Blessèd are you who second guess

Blessèd you sheep who wandered, who wouldn't mind
Blessèd the ones who've been left behind

Blessèd who trusts in the frightening bird
Some say this blessing can't be earned

Some press their blessed ears to the black ground
the blessing to catch what can be found

Some blessings wear an angel's robe,
have janky teeth, fearsome eyes,
then dissolute into mere molecules,
tiny dust motes
floating up to the sky

Hear us!

Our seven and a half billion mouths call out for fat loaves.

Fear not. Ha!

Blessèd lambs, Blessèd muck.

Blessèd are you

At least as blessed as us.

O God

I stand outside of my office looking up
neck pinched tight as an arrow

O daughter-shaped cloud pitched forward
asking for a spot on the couch
so she can make a rainbow
of her body

O cloud-shaped son-pile, two rolling raccoons,
claws backbending into blue

I stare at this holier cathedral ceiling
exhale saying *this is beautiful*

O God of that rainbow
O slick bow of their bodies

Yesterday, a student told me a story
of campers with Froot-loop
and macaroni necklaces,
dingy knees—How he had heard
that their young bodies
were cleaved,
bows bent in the hands of a sick
counselor, someone they trusted,
a man my student, too,
had known,
and also had trusted

Later, in Arby's, with my sons,
my daughter, we watched
over sliders and a tray of fries,
the TV—Saw a line of women,

five sisters, give their testimonies,
pour words through their mouths
with tears streaking into them

Women heart-pierced by arrows,
and those Pennsylvanian priests,
hundreds and hundreds of girls
bent low to snap
under their holy hands

Can we still love this world?
There is no small tremor
of our murmuring
that can refuse what's holy
under the crack
of a cloud's lip

Or a daughter's body made rainbow
instead of a snuffed-out wick

What rises up
after the campground,
wet-wrong with lake water?

Where are we left
in our looking,

Lord

and what spell can we conjure?

CAST

moon bright in the bone house
moon loves the bone spouse

moon slipped into bone stew
moon sifted for bone roux

moon bowl, bone cup
sky's crumbs heaped up

bone light in the moon swing
moon slung in the bone tree

moon drunk off bone beer
little moon the bone fears

moon heart knocked from bone table
moon speaks a bone fable

moon clench of bone fist
moon-cheek bone-kissed

moon-white of bone's eye
moon towel the bone dry

moon broke bone curse
moon longs for bone nurse

bone-hard moon shin
moon lost, bone wins

moon gone bone dark
moon music in bone's bark

moon high bone flute
moon wrung bone mute

moon's maybe, bone's yes
moon gold in bone chest

bone break into star shard
moon sword of bone-guard

it's a moon snow in the bone-cold
swallow the moon, you'll never get old

a moon hoop, bone's toy
what's a moon but forgotten joy

moon green, bone sick
moon salt, bone lick

moon field with bone-stalk
moon whisper bone talk

moon penny is bone money
moon gin laced with bone honey

moon groan the bone birth
moon asks, *what's the bone worth?*

moonshine in the bone shed
moon's yeast makes the earliest bread

To Heaven in a Whirlwind
2 Kings 2:11-12

Enough of fire, of pseudo-prophet or fakey priest. I've kept
lists of what was lost, years where people must have dug wells
iridescent under a heavyhanded heat. Some families have too many
jars remain empty, children still. I wonder
again if praying three or seven times will be enough.
        Measure. Lacking. Bow slowly.
How heavy. Can we fault the ones who turn knives
        from their ribcage to the tree? Carve, then set

the tall Asherah poles up? Their mouths are also caked
after years of not even a drop of dew. Ask, ask again.
        Now ask again. Their
Kings did the evil. The
eye of the Lord is snapped tight.
None of them see heaven coming, even while flames
        scorch eyebrows, wheel wells blink through golden
        dusk. Whirlwind
upends dead stalks, chaffblind
people peer out of their huts while his shadowman Elisha
        refuses again

to leave his side. *Be quiet.* Elijah is rolling up his cloak to
open the river like a zipper, keep his and his successor's feet dry.

How these things could have actually happened is
        beside the point. Some
eye gleamed over a candle and wrote this version of the story down.
A double portion, that's what Elisha asks for. Caveat,
        he'll only get it if... Let's
veer back to the road ashcoated from the recent chariot's fire.
        Where the shape of the man used to be.
        Whose profit, Elijah? Why you, not them, not me?

Even Elisha asked, *Where is the Lord? The God of Elijah?*
  from the epicenter of his grief.
Now tell me how does his question, unlike those who came before,
    and mine which come after,
      end in a doubled blessing, not in a test, or a crispy pyre,
      not in his own dead blood?

Beloved

Sometimes it's you in the raven's beak. Passed
for meat, for bread. Some light strained, wanes down hall
way. The gleam of afternoon. You stalled, last
late. Your hunched minutes as crumbs, given out all

crusts, your hours answer the same, lame questions.
You pass yourself lightly into the mouths
of the young. Numb, they swallow you: lessons
all your fortitude, pilled gravel ground down

under your feet. Pebbles in your shoes. You make
copies. Spreadsheets. Your kindness is printed
in stacks of twenty, thirty. You drop from beak, a steak.
Fear that it will be in vain. Sustenance

comes for you too, friend; look and see the black
birds circling, just ahead above the fence.

Nobody's Mother

it's nice here because you are a nobody

you like the silence and first softness of morning
call it your dark mercenary friend   (you pay by the
day)

watch yourself draw circles in the woodchips while the
kids are playing
they are chasing each other with sticks
          today they go nowhere interesting
          you warn them repeatedly

    you only have two eyes!

there is your fruit   you who feel fruitless
you who love paper flowers made by tiny human hands

plates printed with potato stamps

you who are savage when you throw them away
              you throw them away

sitting on this bench you tell yourself *the end isn't
          written yet*
you covet Kroger's purple orchids planted in ceramic
          pots,
how god made them so precious they make you cry
as you roll through with the cart, its gimpy squeaking
          wheel

plastic carton of feta   boxes of macaroni and cheese
dollar cans of beans   tortillas   milk
tubs of yogurt   frozen peas

you want to be reborn as a laser-beam   galactic
          and expansive
to feel as if you take up space   are space
instead of just some body picking up the space
          throwing old undies in the hamper
tossing metal cars in the bin

you know then with certainty you are a dot that won't
          connect
your brain fragile and oh so very human
all the facts shake around in you like unrolled mints
          all the dates erased   names you used to
know
you were young   you know you were young once
you know you were

          you blame the media the scrolling the much
disrupted REM

          you blame yourself

          you blame the way the night keeps coming up over
the horizon

          you blame him sometimes too

          you desire breath (a holy scroll unfolded and rolled
up again)

          and
from the bench

          you pray

call out to God who you've named *The Pocket of Most*

Things or
Tree I Come to Hoping for Answers or *That Distant Thread*
or

that's it

your want   your want   hums mutely
rolled like socks in overfilled drawers

hear the familiar ding of a timer you do not remember
setting

> holy Holy   won't you have mercy   save us
> from the diction of distraction dis-assemble
> dis-assemble   dis-assemble us

see, now you are a woman in a mirror

a woman shining back at herself

a penny picked up and pocketed

nestled tightly in a daughter's sweaty palm

God the daughter
God the mother-maker
God who is a single perfect orchid in the shape of a heart

Anticipation

Angels dusty in
near morning, titmouse under
tender straw. Pebbled light and
inside her body a
calm broke. She anticipates
incandescent blood drying on her thighs.
Paper-thin, the space between his skin
and hers, she will read all the answers in the black stones of his eyes.
Shifted now, she brings him closer,
inhales the tang
of God, this
normal girl, in normal, human dark.

praxis, too

a resurrection of Wendy Xu's "praxis"

When I had my reach towards malice, against you without description

(War, a white hand) (Earth fabric)

The numbers of time, the anyone of it

A fear pastoral, pined for

Do imagine thorn your poem

Do clean your want; blue what you are

Does newness, not satisfaction, push me over equally?

The will of finite writing, our arms an oration

Be out, you concentric eye, you sound, you put-down

Water's tedious margin, the inventory of me was the fantasy

And the done world down, not taken up

Act of rebellion's closing (good one)

Blue of the space ring I lie in, I move into, through, out of

see the

> preposterous
> tiny shoulder
> shakes leaves make

they reach into time-
not-time-yet— right
now it is bright,

a low sky like
pale rib-skin laced
with cloud's purple

scrim—let's dissect
any thought that
can't slice clean, pound

cake sans icing—
O what a sweet,
fat morning

came again—felt
unlikely—but
you know tomorrow

will come too, hold it loose,
maybe some rain,

maybe dancing

Mary Ruefle Told Me

that the sun's vitamin D absorbs more quickly through the tongue,
she said this with hers stuck out, in between the reading of her poems.
Her hair puffed off her head in brown clouds, she sat balanced like a
       turnip
on a stool at the front of the classroom, and to tell you the truth, she
       didn't say
this extraordinary thing just to me, there were a bunch of us listening,
flat-faced as root vegetables, numbed over from days of lectures,
       readings.

This was years ago, and I remember her saying what she loves most,
the thing we should all try, was to stand in the cold woods
and turn her whole body to face the sun, an act of worship
shot through with green and yellow light, and also, what the hell,
it's just fun. She said she would stick her silly muscle out for at least
fifteen seconds, counting vitamins, tasting the cold,
lapping joyfully at the beams of the sun.

My friend Anna Lee says the morning sun is best for fighting
what's seasonal and depressed but how many mornings
of early sun would I need to combat this sodden, wrung out year?

Today the coffee tree at the top of the hill has a thousand tongues
and shakes gently under a morning sun, the first in weeks.
It's cold, and my heart has been colored such a long stretch of gray.
What if I had a thousand tongues to turn outward towards my uplift?
What if I remembered how to shake my body, turn to what I need?

All of a sudden, I want to run the rest of the mile to my office,
but the fact of the matter is I'm carrying an extra bag,
and it is full of books, so instead, I stick my tongue all the way out
and count to fifteen, then to twenty, while I keep walking all the way
to thirty-seven, and I don't stop until I reach where I'm going.

We Came Running

Her body was the raven's beak, black-gold,
yawning, carrying him as bread. Skin glowed
aureate in lantern light, yeasty after-
birth in straw. She was cracked open, lowly
egg sans yolk. Rustle of black feathers,
the dark nest she'd made. They'd been, most
likely, alone, when she'd wiped his heathered
face of its caul, watched his lips call nighthost,
pitched to angels hovering. Them swiftly gone,
shot from that low margin into whitespace.
How many minutes. What hour, eons
alone no more. We came running. The face
of the star witnessed a loaf new risen, the
whole mouth of the world opening, slowly.

Mite

Around a marble tabletop
father, mother, daughter,
sons. Birthday gifts having already
been given over morning bowls,
they eat their taco salad now,
while mourning doves
and the neighbor's dogs
chaos the yard. Almost sunset,
late March. Before the van was loaded,
the bikes and books and beds
given away. Before the new job
fell apart. The boy, newly eleven,
turns his face as each person gives
the actual gift, *listen as we*
tell you what it is we love:
you, a reader, you, a funny boy,
you, so smart and perceptive,
you, a good brother, you,
the best of friends. The boy,
not shy, says thank you, thank you
in his slipshod way, through his comic
teeth. Nods and shines like a candle
in a cake. The family moves after
into the living room and the mother
wipes at the corners of her eyes, reminds
each to carry dishes to the sink.
The dishwasher, loaded, hymns.
The table, an altar wiped clean.

The Lord Appears to _____

See the crest, lean across the breach.
        What second skin needs to be pulled
        back, so the shimmer of holiness can break?

How can we savor the solemn bee hum
        of a spoken, not dulled, presence?
        Hush, it is here that we are newly made.

Finally unafraid to ask, we make supplicant
        of ourselves, imagine a response:

So what if what we ask is also spent,
        lent to the next guy? O, we are poor,
        so human. Always groaning. Our faces

Shine and are shadowed in all our body's windows.
        See our temples of cut glass,
        with their gleaming cedar beams.

Walk with me, Love, the Creator says.
        O, our Name will be placed here
        forever. Our Eyes see.

The human heart is not built or kept
        as easily as a temple. But we were
        under the impression we could hold

Each joist like a pencil, try to write us
        where we wouldn't fade.
        We know, though, in our guts,
        that the future can't be bought, or held, is but a shade.

We hear, but do not always understand.
        How much clearer could it be?
        Ask, knock.
        We hold up ours. These human hands.

Agnus Dei

A caught hoof who takes away my shame.
Gamey bit of fluff, flicked into spark, lighting a survivor's fire.
        You are
never lost. I am herd. Mote, member, being, among, one of.
        Belong to me, to
us, in our unbelief.
Some songs sing themselves.

Deeper in the cave, now, I'll listen for your softest bleats. I am
eager, and
I hope you can hear me.

SHUTTLE

Who threw all that robust confetti into the trees overnight? Burnt toffee, magenta, bloodroot. What thrums at the edge of a pasture, a thin country stretch called Short Shun, a one lane bridge.

The margin. Like, above the rush of the road could an astronaut tilting her face sideways to get a better eyeball on the earth see each leaf cluster, see us coming now through the mist pocket, how the morning's foam has gone cold?

Pull up a chair, Mama, this picture's for you, my daughter says, when she hands me the moon, cratered with grey pepperoni and her name perfect, all caps and underlined. *P-H-Y-L-L-I-N-A* tilted around the circumference of her picture like a question.

Who is swiftly disappearing? Whose twin is balanced now in the sky like a thimble on an ochre plate? *Morning, God*! I can see us spinning there over the field, steady as chameleons, the leaves like orange eyes looking: look at us, how we are.

The corn stalks have already been broken. And we are still sunburnt from summer, and gathered together, passing by changing trees.

Kristina Erny is a third-culture poet who grew up in South Korea and elsewhere abroad. She holds an MFA from the University of Arizona. Her work has won the Tupelo Quarterly Poetry Prize and the Ruskin Art Club Poetry Award. Her poems have appeared in *The Los Angeles Review, Yemassee, Blackbird, Southern Humanities Review*, and *Tupelo Quarterly*, among other journals. She lives with her husband and kids in Shanghai.

www.ingramcontent.com/pod-product-compliance
Lightning Source LLC
Chambersburg PA
CBHW032050040426
42449CB00007B/1047